Runs of Life

Ernest Dempsey

Modern History Press

Ann Arbor, MI

Runs of Life
Copyright © 2019 by Ernest Dempsey. All Rights Reserved.

Library of Congress Cataloging-in-Publication Data

Names: Dempsey, Ernest, 1977- author.
Title: Runs of life / Ernest Dempsey.
Description: Ann Arbor, MI : Modern History Press, [2019].
Identifiers: LCCN 2019000128 (print) | LCCN 2019000858 (ebook) | ISBN
  9781615994410 (Kindle, ePub, pdf) | ISBN 9781615994397 (pbk. : alk. paper)
  | ISBN 9781615994403 (hardcover : alk. paper)
Classification: LCC PR9540.9.D46 (ebook) | LCC PR9540.9.D46 A6 2019 (print) |
  DDC 821/.92--dc23
LC record available at https://lccn.loc.gov/2019000128

Published by
Modern History Press
5145 Pontiac Trail
Ann Arbor, MI 48105

www.ModernHistoryPress.com
info@ModernHistoryPress.com
tollfree 888-761-6268
fax 734-663-6861

To Kaloo,
who runs free in memories

Contents

Preface

Running is natural—an act combining freedom of motion and personal energy to take one's body and spirit out of the "normal" mode of movement. We run early in our lives, starting in childhood. Nobody needs to teach it to us. Even before we are able to muster the strength and attain the balance for running with our bodies, our spirit is long familiar with running. There truly is something special about running.

The themed poems in this publication come mainly from personal memories of running—out of simple play and childhood fun time, at times for safety, or even in dreams. I loved running; still love it though now I don't get many "calls" for speeding up my feet and setting my pace to that level of energy. But I do run, body and soul. So why poems about running?

Because I feel running gives us strength and confidence that last long after our legs stop or switch to the walking mode. Each run is an act of asserting one's personal power—of the ability to leave things behind and move on, even if we know it's momentary. Whenever we run, in body or spirit, we are in the race; we are up for it—for expressing the life in us. Running has its rhythm just like poetry. Poetry is a medium of expression as running is an expression of life.

I hope my *Runs of Life* bring you memories of your running life and these poems resonate with the confidence and the personal strength that keep our lives active and hopeful.

On Top of the World

Clouds, wind, an open ground
We ran in play that afternoon
The time from called-off classes our boon
Tireless feet, unending noise of joy
Innocent hearts racing around
No bell or teacher, no classroom walls
On top of the world lay our ground
We ran with every stop erased

Me and the Bee

Back to my room for a nap
A walk in scorching sun, until
My cap shook a twig overhead
My back stung-startled me
No arguing with buzzing
My feet took the lead
Away from angry bees I ran
One kept me company all the way
I had to hide me in the bush
Getting a moment of peace
"Good Job!" I told my legs
No words though for my cap!

A Small Miracle

"The TV's not working," I tell my brother
"What to do?" His eyes expand behind his glasses
We've just arrived at Gramma's house
Ten minutes to our beloved show
We could wait for a miracle, or
Make it happen ourselves
"We run back home," I say
We see our challenge, he nods
Step in step we run together
The fields, the cemetery, the afternoon sky
Witness our spirit of boyhood
Covering the mile back home
In time we get to our house
The show's just started
We win our challenge
The miracle happens

Screen of Innocence

No walls are there to stop
Excited kids playing outside
Chasing each other on winding paths
Running across lush happy fields
The town's peace still breathing
Music of chirping birds in the air
Cheering farmers and the quietly grazing cattle
Gasping, heart thumping, I run
Living my later childhood adventure
Lighting the screen of innocence

She's No More!

Mom screams outside – I'm startled
My brother runs into my room
"Auntie's dead!" His face is pale
The world's changed in a second
Still and speechless, I stay home
Can't hold myself in a place though
Childbirth – why it kills?
Stepping outside, I run across the fields
My sweet aunt's gone – I run
Hoping the news would be mere rumor
In hope of seeing her alive – I run
Oblivious to the ground, my feet know
I get there at her house
They tell me she's no more
I leave and run back
Heading toward my grandma's house
My cousins there all teary
On a happier day
We run together in laugh and play
Today it's time to sit and mourn

Runs of Life

Born with weaker hind legs
Kaloo, our canine chum, flashed on calling
Fast as lightning all around the run
Where we spent fun summer afternoons
His swirling tail, our laughter, water's flow
No music could be sweeter, no harmony as perfect
The creek's there today
No Kaloo – he rests in peace
Thousands of miles away I sit
Counting the runs of life I had
Thinking also of those to come
Along the stretch of time unseen

Racing Heart

More urgency, still somewhat fun
Catching the bus early to board a flight
Brisk walk won't do, says clock on the phone
The morning road's free of noise
Inviting me to test my vigor
No reason not to take this call
I let my feet tap on the road
Dancing to the music of beat and breath
I win my challenge, my vigor proved
But my heart won't stop when I do

Hearts Dead and Buried

Putting on personas
Why pretend?
Racing against time
Won't erase the end

Your heart is wild
Racing against time
Hearts dead and buried
Lie still in rhyme

Out of the rat race
Hearts dead and buried
Make promises of peace
Neither kept nor carried
Walking through fire
Make promises of peace
Saving a red drop
Melting frigid seas

Between Hearts and Horizons

Out of the walls
Around the house
Across the fence
Along new, self-defined paths
Places between hearts and horizons
Low or high
Races run with loved ones
Somber dreams of lives past
Echoes of laughter and sobs
Tears leaving strained eyes
A spirit half-human half-divine
Leading to new starting points
Waving at eternal waves
Stretched from beat to wild clouds

Bison's Final Day Out

Free from the farm
Free from fate in days to come
Fifteen heavy healthy bison ran

Continuing across the streets and lake
Chased by anxious, scared men
Scared – with cars, radios, guns

Gift of nature, the bison ran
Living their day beyond fences
Making their way to the wild

The captors couldn't stand this run
They shot the bison one by one
Ending their life, not their freedom

About the Author

Ernest Dempsey edits the quarterly journal *Recovering the Self* (www.recoveringself.com/) published from Michigan. He has published four books including his story book *The Blue Fairy and Other Tales of Transcendence* (Modern History Press, 2010). His poetry book *Two Candles* has just been published. He has also worked as a citizen journalist and a freelance proofreader and editor. Dempsey is vegetarian and an animal rights activist. He runs a popular blog *Word Matters!* at www.ernestdempsey.com/.

A thought-provoking excursion to life's last breath

Ernest Dempsey's second collection of short stories *The Blue Fairy* takes a subject that has been dreaded for centuries – 'Death'. It is one of the few works of fiction, which neither treats the subject as the 'D word' by bringing in fantasies of afterlife nor compromises the solemnity by trying to evaporate the reality of death in humor. Instead, Dempsey explores the many sides to the subject that make the final departure a meaningful reality of existence. Inspired mostly by real life experiences, Dempsey's *The Blue Fairy* ingeniously integrates dying with living. It is a book for the soul.

~ ~ ~

"There is something about the somberness of his search for moral principles that reminds me of Victorian poets such as Tennyson, Bronte, Kipling, and Hardy writing in the 19th century. Bringing these themes into 21st century views is an interesting task."

—Janet Grace Riehl, *Village Wisdom*

Modern History Press